DAWSON ᴛʜᴇ DOLPHIN

TULSA

ISBN: 978-1-957262-28-4

Dawson the Dolphin

Yorkshire Publishing

1425 E 41st Pl
Tulsa, OK 74105
www.YorkshirePublishing.com
918.394.2665

Published in the USA

DAWSON

～ THE ～

DOLPHIN

A Story about Bottlenose Dolphins

#3 in the *Under the Sea* Series

By

Adrienne Palma

To Michael, David, Chris, and Ann

Dream BIG

Foreword

Adrienne Palma has once again written an engaging and educational book to bring young readers into the natural world. From her experiences with the Outer Banks Dolphin Research Project, to her visit to Dolphin Research Center, she brings an understanding of the importance of both wild dolphin research and marine mammal facilities. Through Dawson's story, children are able to learn about dolphin biology and conservation in a fun way, and understand the important role that marine mammal facilities like Dolphin Research Center play in providing a forever home to animals in need.

Emily Guarino
Director of Research Training & Data Collection
Dolphin Research Center
Marathon, Florida

Hi, my name is Dawson. I am a bottlenose dolphin.

Come for a swim as I tell you my story.

I was born off the coast of North
Carolina two years ago.

I am grey with a torpedo-shaped body that helps
me glide swiftly through the ocean. My mouth
is curved so it looks like I am always smiling.

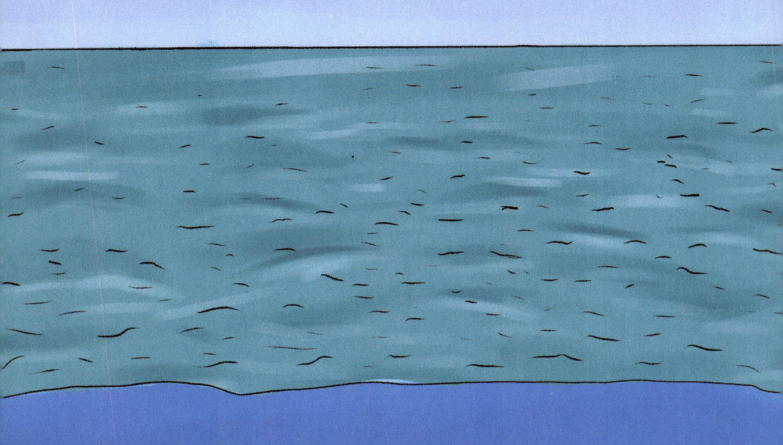

I spent my days swimming around with other
dolphins. The group or pod I swam with
was constantly changing. My friends Poppy,
Tucker, and I stayed together for several
months. We loved playing together.

I like to squawk, leap high in the air, and slap my tail on the surface of the water!

I love to blow bubbles too!

Did you know that every dolphin has its own special whistle? This whistle is used for identification, similar to a human's name.

I have really good hearing. Certain sounds
travel from my lower jaw to my inner
ear, which sends signals to my brain.

I can see well in and out of the water too. Even though I live underwater, I must come up to the surface to breathe air.

One day I saw scientists on a boat taking photographs of me. They took photographs of my dorsal fin and looked for distinctive markings. They were keeping track of where I was swimming and the water temperature.

For a few days, I had not been feeling well. I was not eating anything and was swimming slowly.

One of the scientists noticed I was sick as I swam alongside the research boat.

The scientist contacted the local
stranding response network.

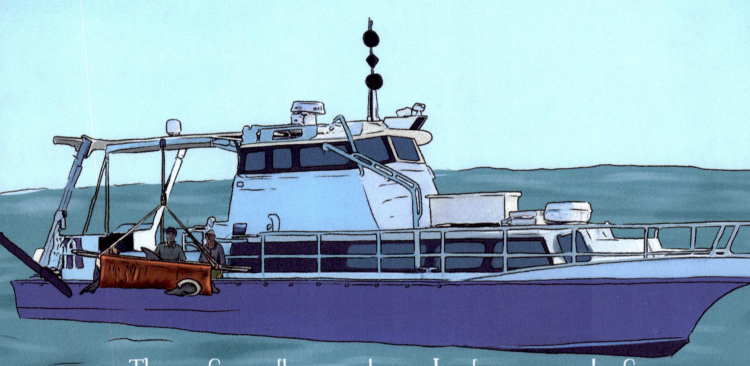

These friendly people picked me up out of
the water and placed me onto their boat.

They transferred me to a rehab
facility in Florida to get better.

I stayed there for a few months, gaining
strength and getting healthy again.

Then I was taken to the Dolphin Research Center in Grassy Key, Florida because I was too young to be released back to the wild. Many people donated money so that I could live here.

This center also provides sanctuary for sea lions, tortoises, and exotic birds!

I now spend my days at the Dolphin Research
Center swimming in the waters off the Gulf
of Mexico. I love the friendly trainers!

They call my name, give me high 5's on my flippers, and clap a lot! The people who work here really love us dolphins!

All of the dolphins here receive excellent care.

We get lots of yummy fish to eat!

Even though dolphins get water from the fish eaten, the trainers give us extra water as needed.

We stay hydrated!

The researchers keep lots of data about us.
The Dolphin Research Center uses the
same type of database so that other
scientists and researchers can compare
notes about us. Isn't that awesome!

Thanks for joining me for a swim today.

I love my forever home.

Right now, my new friend Jax and I are showing off our acrobatic skills to some excited children. Wait until they see how high we can jump out of the water!

Fun Facts

a.   Bottlenose dolphins have an average lifespan of 29 years.

b.   They are 7-9 feet long and can weigh over 600 pounds.

c.   They can travel up to 25 miles an hour

d.   They can hold their breath for just over 7 minutes.

e.   Dolphins also produce high frequency clicks, which act as a sonar system called echolocation (ek-oh-low-KAY-shun). When the clicking sounds hit an object in the water, like a fish or rock, they bounce off and come back to the dolphin as echoes. Echolocation tells the dolphins the shape, size, speed, distance, and location of the object.

f.   Male dolphins are called "bulls." Females are called "cows." Young dolphins are called "calves" and stay alongside their mothers between 3-6 years.

g.   The Orca, also known as the killer whale, is a type of dolphin.

h.   Bottlenose dolphins shed their outermost layer of skin every 2 hours.

i.   Bottlenose Dolphins have distinctive skin markings that help camouflage them from potential predators. Their tails have two horizontal paddles called "flukes" which contain no bones or muscles.

j.   Their elongated upper and lower jaws give them their name of Bottlenose.

k.   Bottlenose dolphins are gentle and friendly, however, they can defend themselves. They have natural predators, like sharks.

l.   *Author's Note:*

   - *For the purposes of this story, Dawson is jumping out of the water in the sound of North Carolina. The water is too shallow for dolphins to jump.*

   - *Dawson was rescued while in the water. Dolphins are usually not spotted appearing sick at sea. Many are found either stranded ashore or foundering in shallow waters.*

   - *The background scenes showcase the beauty of the Outer Banks. Note the Bodie Island Lighthouse (cover and p.4); the duck blind (p.7); the Marc Basnight Bridge (p. 8); the osprey nest (p.11); and the pelicans on Bird Island (p.12).*

References and Resources

Bottlenose dolphins

https://www.nationalgeographic.com/animals/mammals/c/common-bottlenose-dolphin/

https://kids.nationalgeographic.com/animals/mammals/bottlenose-dolphin/

https://www.natgeokids.com/uk/discover/animals/sea-life/dolphins/

https://animalcorner.org/animals/bottlenose-dolphins/

https://kidsanimalsfacts.com/bottlenose-dolphin-facts-for-kids/

https://easyscienceforkids.com/all-about-dolphins/#:~:text=Bottlenose%20dolphins%20live%20in%20rivers%20and%20coastal%20areas,for%20Kids%20Most%20dolphins%20are%20black%20or%20gray.

https://biologydictionary.net/bottlenose-dolphin/

https://www.ammpa.org/sites/default/files/files/animalfactsheets/AMMPA-DolphinFactSheet-FINAL-Web.pdf

https://onlinelibrary.wiley.com/doi/full/10.1111/mms.12601

https://oceana.org/marine-life/common-bottlenose-dolphin/

Dolphin Research

Dolphin Research Center (Grassy Key, FL)
https://dolphins.org/

Nags Head Dolphin Watch Tours
https://www.nagsheaddolphinwatch.com/

Marine Animal Safety

To report a stranded or injured marine animal, there is a Dolphin and Whale 911 App
https://www.fisheries.noaa.gov/report

Acknowledgements

This book was so much fun to research and write! The most fun was having the opportunity to swim with the dolphins at the Dolphin Research Center in Grassy Key, Florida!!!

Many people near and far were involved in making this book a reality. Heartfelt thanks to each of you for taking precious time to answer my many questions and provide suggestions to make this story factual.

- Emily Guarino, Director of Research Training & Data Collection, Dolphin Research Center, many thanks for writing the Foreword and for your support and guidance throughout this adventure. I am indebted to you!

- Celie Florence and the dedicated staff at the Dolphin Research Center. You made my visit a trip of a lifetime! Many thanks for all you do for these animals. You are amazing!!!

- Mary Stella, Director of Media & Marketing, Dolphin Research Center, you have definitely been my go to person!

- Barbara and John Sibunka, proofreaders and fact checkers extraordinaire!

- Cathy Evanoff, good friend and techie extraordinaire, thanks for keeping the website up to date!

- Samantha Ryan and the great team at Yorkshire Publishing! Number 3 in the series and still going strong!!!

To you readers, thank you for selecting this book. The writing of this book and the upcoming books in the *Under the Sea* series is letting me live my dream everyday.

Dream BIG...then make it happen

Also by Adrienne Palma

Roza Sanchez
Living the Dream
Under the Sea series
Lola the Loggerhead
Shalim the Shark

Coming Soon...

The 4th book in the *Under the Sea* series:

Crystal the Crab

A Story About Ghost Crabs

By Adrienne Palma

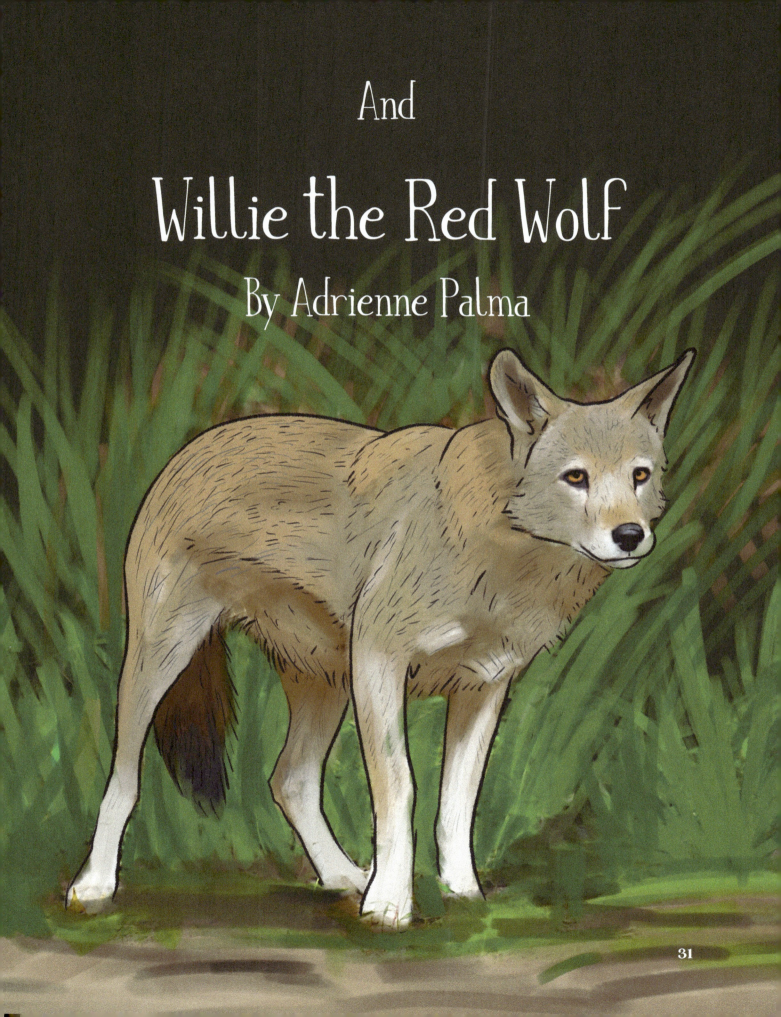

And

Willie the Red Wolf

By Adrienne Palma

CPSIA information can be obtained
at www.ICGtesting.com
Printed in the USA
LVHW072045050723
751603LV00014B/250